Credit Repair Guide

How To Fix Credit Score and Remove Negatives from Credit Report

By Smart Reads

Free Audiobook

As a thank you for being a Smart Reader you can choose 2 FREE audiobooks from audible.com.
Simply sign up for free by visiting
www.audibletrial.com/Travis to get your books.

Visit:
www.smartreads.co/freebooks
to receive Smart Reads books for FREE

Check us out on Instagram:
www.instagram.com/smart_readers
@smart_readers

ABOUT SMARTREADS

Choose Smart Reads and get smart every time. Smart Reads sorts through all the best content and condenses the most helpful information into easily digestible chunks.

We design our books to be short, easy to read and highly informative. Leaving you with maximum understanding in the least amount of time.

Smart Reads aims to accelerate the spread of quality information so we've taken the copyright off everything we publish and donate our material directly to the public domain. You can read our uncopyright below.

We believe in paying it forward and donate 5% of our net sales to Pencils of Promise to build schools, train teachers and support child education.

To limit our footprint and restore forests around the globe we are planting a tree for every 10 hardcover books we sell.

Thanks for choosing Smart Reads and helping us help the planet.

Sincerely,

Travis & the Smart Reads Team

Uncopyright 2017 by Smart Reads. No rights reserved worldwide. Any part of this publication may be reproduced or transmitted in any form without the prior written consent of the publisher.

Disclaimer: The publisher and author make no representations or warranties with respect to the accuracy or completeness of these contents and disclaim all warranties for a particular purpose. The author or publisher is not responsible for how you use this information. The fact that an individual or organization is referred to in this document as a citation or source of information does not imply that the author or publisher endorses the information that the individual or organization provided.
.

TABLE OF CONTENTS

Introduction	2
Chapter 1: What Does a Credit Report Contain?	7
Chapter 2: What is a FICO Score?	9
Chapter 3: How Can You Order Free Credit Reports?	19
Chapter 4: How Mistakes Appear on Your Credit Report	22
Chapter 5: Removing Errors from Your Own Credit Report	23
Chapter 6: Remove Every Negative Item from Your Report	26
Chapter 7: Steps You Can Take to Ensure All Negative Items are Removed	29
Chapter 8: How to Handle Collection Agencies	37
Chapter 9: Another Method of Legally Removing Negative Items	39
Chapter 10: What Mistakes You Should Avoid When Fixing Your Credit?	45

INTRODUCTION

This book is based on information and experience taken from reputable people working in the business of financial planning for close to 20 years and also as mortgage brokers for a period of time. It includes clear and easy information on what to do and what not to do when it comes to cleaning up your credit score.

Financial planners often have clients who come to them for advice before purchasing any valuable asset such as a house or a car. They must assist clients to correct their credit, not only because it's part of their job to do so but also because many have a deep loyalty to their clients and also their families. In doing so, clients would be able to correct a credit report that would then enable them to receive better interest rates and save more money. This is a service a few of them provide for free, however, the satisfaction it brings them is enormous and the clients remain loyal. Being able to correct mistakes or inaccuracies on a credit report can be easy even if you do it yourself. The following information is on how to clean up a credit report containing negative items. Negative items on your credit report can ruin your chances or stop you from buying your new car, the house you want, or getting a new credit card.

Credit card companies and lawyers will often charge large amounts to get this done for you. However, the truth is, you can do it on your own and it won't cost you anything – except some time and a bit of effort.

The time of paying enormous fees for this particular service is over. Most books sold on this subject today just refer the reader to their own website or to a credit restoration business which then comes with a substantial price tag. This book will let you in on the secrets used by professionals who will charge you a lot of money for this type of service.

I learned information on how to correct credit ratings in a legal and permanent way from a lawyer who would charge $1500 - $3000 for these services. And that was several years ago. The price would only have gone up.

The lawyer I learned all this from had assisted a client to get her credit restored. It was at 528 to a FICO score of 689. A FICO score is a method used to assess credit risk and will be discussed in detail further on. She was able to get approval for the loan the lawyer helped her get at a better rate. She saved around $380 on her mortgage per month because of it. Without the higher FICO score the client would have paid a lot more. She paid the lawyer more than $2500 for the service but when I told her that this was too much money, her response was that not correcting her credit would have meant she would pay $125,000 more over the entire life of her loan. This would take her another 30 years to pay off.

Once her credit was fixed, she received a much lower rate of interest on her credit cards which helped pay off higher interest that she had. The client also returned a car she was leasing and leased a better car for much less. This then saved her on the car premium and homeowner insurance. This was hundreds of dollars of savings each month.

Around 10 years later, this client had more than $100,000 in an investment account. It wasn't spent on creditors because of bad credit so she was able to save this for herself. The client's daughter then started college and the client used part of the money to buy a house close to the college. The four-bedroom home was used to house several other female students who of course, paid rent, which in turn paid the mortgage, leaving around $260 a month for the daughter's spending money.

Once the client's daughter completed her studies, the house was sold and they made a $55,000 profit on it. This client then reinvested this money.

Of course, not all credit stories are like this one, but the money saving difference between having bad credit and having good credit is massive. It can easily add up to savings of thousands of dollars per year.

This book isn't about quick re-scoring, which you must have so you can prove that a credit bureau has made an error. In such a case, you would need to prove this and provide all documentation to do so. If you cannot do this it will be denied. This too is an expensive process.

You also don't need cash for payment on your credit cards in order to decrease your debt percentage. This is also utilized for quick re-scoring oftentimes. What it actually is, is filing electronically with the bureau to have mistakes deleted, or to report a change in your debt ratio quickly. Usually this would mean you need to have some extra cash to get it done. It will calculate it quite quickly (around 5 to 7 business days) and you won't have to wait one or two months for creditors to show payments.

Within these pages you'll find guidance on how to legally eliminate every negative item from a credit report. Today, the process is a lot simpler and more advanced than years ago. What you have to do is understand and know exactly what steps to take so credit bureaus don't refuse your requests.

If any of these things appear on your individual credit report, keep reading: collection accounts, repos, bankruptcies, charge offs, judgments, loan modifications, short sales, late payments or other negative items. If your credit is perfect you don't need to read any more.

For your everyday living expenses and necessities it is vital that you keep a good FICO score.

You need to figure out if:
• You are paying more than you should for your car insurance,
• You are paying a lot more than you should for rental or homeowner's insurance,
• You have been rejected for a credit card,
• A lender has declined your mortgage,

- You are charged a higher rate because of your particular credit score,
- An employer won't hire or promote you because of bad credit,
- You cannot keep a professional license because of your Fico score,
- You are paying too much for the mortgage, care, insurance and also credit cards every month.

Fixing your credit will save you thousands each year. You could then invest that money or save it, take a vacation, or just have some extra money to do something you enjoy.

CHAPTER 1: WHAT DOES A CREDIT REPORT CONTAIN?

Credit reporting agencies will format and report the information mentioned below differently, however, the same basic information categories will appear in all of them.

Identifying Information
This information includes: your birth date, social security number, and employment information. These are not utilized for the credit scoring. Any updates to the information are derived from the other date that you give to lenders when you apply.

Trade Lines
Trade lines would be any credit accounts you have. Lenders will report on every account that you've set up with them. The lenders report what kind of account it is (for example, mortgage, auto loan, bankcard), the date that you launched the account, the loan amount or credit limit, account balance, as well as what payment history you have.

Credit Inquiries
Whenever you put in an application for any loan, the lender is authorized to obtain your credit report copy. It is in this way that inquiries show on the credit report. This section (Inquiries) displays everyone who has accessed your particular credit report over a two-year period. This report will list "voluntary" inquiries, which come from your request for credit, as well as

"involuntary" inquiries, which would include lenders who ask for your report if they want to send you pre-approved credit offers.

Public Record & Collection Items
Every credit-reporting agency collects information available on public record, which they get from the county and state courts. They also collect information on any overdue debt which they get from the collection agencies. The public record information would include foreclosures, liens, wage attachments, bankruptcies, suits, and also judgments.

CHAPTER 2: WHAT IS A FICO SCORE?

The FICO score is a credit score created by the Fair Isaac Corporation. Both borrowers and lenders use FICO scores as well as other information on a borrower's credit report to evaluate any credit risks and decide whether or not to extend credit. Whenever you apply for any type of credit – mortgage, car loan, credit card, the lenders must know if there's a risk lending you the money. So, a FICO score is a credit score lenders utilize to assess credit risk.

In the United States, you have 3 FICO scores for each credit bureau: TransUnion, Equifax, and Experian. Each of your scores is based upon information that the individual credit bureau has about you in their files. When this type of information changes, so does your credit score. The FICO scores will affect the amount and the terms that a lender will be able to offer you. Improving your FICO score will help your eligibility for better loan and credit rates.

To calculate the 3 FICO scores, all 3-credit reports have to contain one account, at least, and one that's been open 6 months or more. Every report must also contain one account or more that's been updated within the last 6 months. This is to make sure ample, recent information is available in the report so an individual FICO score can be given.

You can head to the site below to check the chart and get a better idea:

http://www.myfico.com/credit-education/whats-in-your-credit-score/

A credit bureau score is also referred to as a FICO score because the majority of scores used by credit bureaus in the United States comes from the software created by Fair Isaac and Company or FICO. All the big credit reporting companies provide the FICO scores to lenders. They are the most reliable resource for determining future credit risks and are solely based on credit report statistics. If the FICO score is high there is less risk.

It is necessary to note however, that there is no score to determine whether an individual will actually be a "bad" or "good" customer. Many lenders utilize FICO scores when making lending decisions but every lender has their own set of strategies, which would include acceptable risk levels for a certain credit product. Not every lender uses the same "cut-off score" and a lot of other factors are used by lenders to determine interest rates for individuals. A FICO score will range between 300 – 850 points. Higher FICO scores mean less risk to lenders and thus lower rates of interest for the individual customer. In some cases, only a few small points difference can mean you'll get a higher or lower interest rate.

For the most part, lenders will need 680 as a FICO score from you so that you can receive a better mortgage rate or loan rate. Even just a few short points below this and you're considered to be a customer with high credit risk. This will mean you'll get a higher interest rate.

There are a lot of different credit data, which compose a FICO score. It can be separated into 5 categories (see below.) Percentages shown in the chart above display the importance of each category when it comes to determining your individual FICO score and whether you are a high or low credit risk.

Payment History comprises the largest percentage, 35%, and gives information on all account payments including, but not limited to:
• Retail accounts, mortgage, credit cards, installment loans, and accounts with finance companies
• Any unfavorable public records such as bankruptcy, suits, wage attachments, collection items, judgments, or delinquency
• The severity of the delinquency
• Past due amounts on collection items or any delinquent accounts
• How much time has passed since delinquency, collection items, unfavorable public records, (if there are any)
• How many past due items appear on your file
• How many accounts have been paid as per agreement

Amounts Owed
• Any amount you owe on accounts
• Any owing amounts on specific account types
• Lack of balance type in certain cases
• How many accounts you have with a lack of balance

- How many accounts you have with balances
- The proportion of the installment loan amount still owing
- The ratio of credit lines that are used (ratio of balances to the total credit limit on revolving accounts)

Credit History Length
- Time from when accounts were opened,
- Time from when accounts were opened, by specific kind of account,
- And time since any account activity was undertaken

New Credit
- The number of accounts recently opened accounts, by account type
- Recent number of credit inquiries
- Time since opening of recent accounts, by account type
- Time since last credit inquiry
- Reinstatement of favorable credit history after past payment issues

Credit Types Utilized
Number of (prevalence, presence, and any recent information) different account types (retail accounts, credit cards, consumer finance accounts, mortgage, installment loans, etc.)

Not Taken Into Consideration with Regards to your Individual FICO Score:

- Your color, race, religion, sex, marital status, and national origin - United States law does not allow credit scoring to take the above facts into consideration, and also any public assistance receipt. If you are using your consumer rights as per the Consumer Credit Protection Act this cannot be taken into account either.
- Age
- Occupation, employer, title, date employed, employment history, salary - Lenders might consider the above information as well as other score types.
- Place of residence
- Interest rates on other accounts or credit cards
- Anything that comes under child or family support or any rental agreements
- Specific inquiry types (requests for credit report) - This score doesn't count inquiries, which are "consumer-initiated" credit report requests you've made so you can check it. The score doesn't count any "promotional inquiries" i.e. lender requests to allow them to offer you "pre-approved" credit offers or any "administrative inquiries" or lender requests to reassess your individual account with them. Any requests marked as originating from employers aren't counted either.
- Information that will not appear in your individual credit report
- Information, which has no predictive use for future credit functioning
- If you are taking part in any type of credit counseling.

Credit Inquiries

If you apply for new credit, will your FICO score fall?

Firstly, it's not likely to drop a lot. It is better not to open several new accounts too quickly as multiple inquiries show on your individual report. Looking to get new credit could be equated with a higher risk; however, the majority of credit scores aren't affected by various inquiries from mortgage, student loan, or auto lenders. They are often treated as a single inquiry therefore will not impact credit scores too much.

What is considered an "Inquiry"?

Applying for credit means you give authorization to lenders to inquire or ask for copies from one of the credit bureaus of your individual credit report. You might notice when you check your report at a later date that the lenders' inquiries have been listed there. Other inquiries might also appear there from businesses you do not know. The inquiries that actually count with regards to your particular FICO score, however, are those that are the result of your new credit applications.

Does an application for new credit affect your FICO score?

Research has shown that when an individual opens a few credit accounts in close succession, then a higher credit risk is usually thought to be the result. Due to this view, a FICO score might be lowered. If you are only shopping around for a better loan rate, it is handled in a different manner and therefore doesn't really affect your FICO score.

Will a credit inquiry (or inquiries) have an affect on my score, and if so by how much?
Applying for new credit will have a different impact for each person. This is based upon everyone's individual credit history. Generally speaking, credit enquiries don't impact a FICO score too much at all – usually it will result in five points or less taken of a FICO score. To give you a better idea of the way it works, the FICO score ranges from 300-850, the highest number being the best possible FICO score to have. Inquiries will have an impact in the case of having a shorter credit history or a few accounts. Going by statistics, an individual who has six or more inquiries, or who has more on credit reports, is more prone to declaring bankruptcy (eight times higher). Inquiries are often used as a way of rating risk, however, they really have a minor role. The really important factors which can affect a FICO score is whether or not you pay all your bills on time as well as your full debt load as shown on your individual credit report.

Are all credit inquiries treated the same way by the formula?
Not every credit inquiry is treated the same. Research shows that FICO scores are better predictors and treated differently when it comes to rate-shopping loans like mortgage, car, or student loans. For those kinds of loans, FICO scores ignore any inquiries made within a 30-day period prior to the scoring. This means if you can find a good loan within thirty days then your inquiries will not affect your FICO score

while you are shopping around for this rate. The FICO score also looks at your report when it comes to inquiries, which are older than thirty days of rate shopping. If there are any, it will count them as one inquiry if they are all within a regular shopping period.

Any FICO scores calculated from an older scoring formula version will look at the period on a 14-day duration. The FICO scores that use the newer scoring formula have a 45-day duration. Every lender will choose the FICO score formula that it would like credit reporting companies to use in order to calculate a FICO score.

Important Things About "Rate Shopping"
If you look around for a student or auto loan, or perhaps a mortgage, it could cause many lenders to ask for your personal credit report despite the fact you're looking for only one loan. The score would ignore mortgage, student and auto loan inquiries made 30 days before scoring, to compensate for that. These inquiries will not affect your FICO score if you happen to find a loan in thirty days. The score also looks at your personal credit report for student, auto, and mortgage loan inquiries which are 30 days or older. If some are found, the inquiries are counted as only 1 inquiry if they fall within the average shopping period. There are older scoring formulas and FICO scores that are calculated from them and consider the shopping period to be 14 days. The newest scoring version formula takes in a 45-day period. Every lender uses whichever FICO scoring formula version they

want credit reporting agencies to use for making calculations.

How to Improve a FICO Score
Should you decide you need to get a loan, make sure you rate shop only within a certain time frame (within 30 days). The FICO scores can differentiate between a single search and many searches for many recent credit lines, partly by the time duration over which the inquiries happen.
Usually, people who have high FICO scoring are consistent with:

- Ensuring bills are paid on time,
- Keeping low balances on their credit cards along with other revolving credit products,
- Applying for and opening new accounts as they are needed.

Below are some practices you can engage in regarding credit management which can help you increase your FICO scores over time:

- If you've had some problems, start re-establishing your individual credit history.
- Open new accounts in a responsible manner and pay them all on time. This will raise the FICO score after a period of time.
- Regularly check your credit reports, in particular, before you apply for any new credit. Make sure everything is up-to-date and accurate. Make sure you order credit reports come from authorized

organizations (like myFICO) so that your inquiries don't negatively affect your score.

CHAPTER 3: HOW CAN YOU ORDER FREE CREDIT REPORTS?

If you want to get access to your credit report for free, here is the official site:

> https://www.annualcreditreport.com

All of the three big credit report bureaus sponsor this site. If you haven't requested your free report within the past 12 months, make sure you do so by going to the website above. Your credit report from Equifax, TransUnion and Experian will be found there.

If you are denied credit at any point you can request your credit report for free if it's done within sixty days of the time you made the inquiry. The particular credit bureau that your credit report used is the one that you'll get the report from. If, for example, you have put in an application for a visa credit card but it was denied, the denial letter will show which particular credit bureau this information was taken from. The bureau's information will also be included. You can either write or you can call them.

What You'll Need:
• Ensure you're within the 60-day period from the inquiry date.
• The name of the agency that has supplied the information; its mailing address, phone number, and website should be in the letter.

- Your name and address, social security number, driver's license (in some states) when you contact the particular bureau.
- The name of the creditor that actually denied the credit and also the date it was denied.

Below are the 3 main credit-reporting bureaus, their mailing addresses and phone numbers if you want a copy of your credit report:

TransUnion
If you want a copy of your report: P.O. Box 390 Springfield, PA 19064 (800) 916-8800
For disputing data in your report: P.O. Box 34012 Fullerton, CA 92634 (800) 916-8800
Reporting credit fraud: (800) 916-8800

Experian
If you want a copy of your report: P.O. Box 8030 Layton, UT 84041 (800) 682-7654
For disputing data in your report: P.O. Box 2106 Allen, TX 75013 (800) 422-4879
Reporting credit fraud: Fax Number (800) 301-7195

Equifax
If you want a copy of your report: P.O. Box 740241 Atlanta, GA 30374-0241 (800) 685-1111
For disputing data in your report: P.O. Box 740256 Atlanta, GA 30374-0256 (800) 216-1035 or (800) 685-5000
Reporting credit fraud: (800) 525-6285

When you have the credit report make sure you assess it carefully. Mistakes often appear on the report so checking it is necessary.

CHAPTER 4: HOW MISTAKES APPEAR ON YOUR CREDIT REPORT

Credit reports that contain errors are often incomplete reports or in some cases even contain information about another individual. This might happen because:

- An individual has applied under several different names for credit i.e. Bob Jones and Robert Jones
- A clerical mistake was made by someone at a bureau or lending facility when reading/entering names and addresses from hand-written applications
- An individual has perhaps given an erroneous social security number
- Credit card or loan payments are accidentally applied to a wrong account
- Social security numbers have been misread by lenders

CHAPTER 5: REMOVING ERRORS ON YOUR CREDIT REPORT

The Fair Credit Reporting Act or (FCRA) has been designed to assist credit bureaus correct and also complete information that goes to businesses so they can use it when they assess an application. Mistakes can be removed easily because the Act requires bureaus to delete any inaccurate information on an individual's credit report.

If you want to remove incorrect information, this is what you'll need:

1. A copy of your individual credit report. This is a must-have.
2. Social security number
3. To identify/highlight in a clear manner every item you dispute on your report.
4. To stick to the facts when explaining the reasons you are disputing the information.
5. To formally request that the erroneous information is removed from your credit report, as per the law.

SAMPLE LETTER FORMAT:

Your Name
Address
City, State, Zip
Date
Complaints Department

The Name of Credit Bureau
Address of Credit Bureau
City, State, and Zip Code
Regarding: Inaccurate information appearing on my credit report.

Dear Sir/Madam,

I am writing in order to dispute certain information, which appears on my personal credit report. Items that I am disputing are underlined on the report - copy attached.
These items are inaccurate and incorrect:
1. Credit account, Account number
2. Creditor, tax court, or judgment.
These items that I have listed are inaccurate and don't belong to me.
Therefore, I request that these items be removed from my report. An investigation and removal of these items would need to be done within the next 30 days according to the Fair Credit Reporting Act. All information that isn't 100% accurate has to be deleted.

Thank you for your assistance with this matter.

Yours Sincerely,
(Signature)
(Your Name)
Enclosed: (List of anything you're enclosing, like a credit report copy)

That credit bureau has to now investigate any mentioned items within 30 days and have them deleted from your particular report unless the bureau can verify the items or your request was found to be frivolous. Once the investigation is done, you should receive a letter about the outcome as well as a new credit report. This new report has to be provided without charge to you. It must also not count against you.

Make sure you send your letter to the particular bureau certified and request a return receipt. Keep your own copy of your letter and receipt.

CHAPTER 6: REMOVING EVERY NEGATIVE ITEM FROM YOUR REPORT

Considering credit bureaus are "for profit" organizations and are private, they must abide by the Fair Credit Reporting Act. They are, after all, a 4 billion dollar business. They have a responsibility to follow any laws that protect the consumers and can only allow negative items on a credit report if they are verifiable and 100% accurate.

When it comes to accuracy, it means that the bureau has a responsibility to ensure all information on a person's credit report is correct, the account opening date is correct, the amounts owed are precise and correct, the account numbers match your individual account number, etc.

Some reports show that credit bureaus often have around 70% errors on report files. There is a good chance that your particular report contains inaccurate information, which you have the right to dispute.

Credit bureaus must also ensure the information reported could be verified by the consumer when it is requested. They must also provide their verification methods and this includes name and address as well as phone numbers of data furnishers if a consumer requests it. They also have to prove that they've received an original and dated contract copy containing your signature.

For the most part, bureaus do comply with the FCRA Act. An automated system is used, most commonly the e-Oscar, a centralized communication tool used for disputes. A dispute is scanned then processed outside of the U.S. where the labor is much cheaper. It is then assigned an e-Oscar two-digit code.

As a consumer, you can request a proof of verification method letter. It is a good idea for you to request a Method of Verification letter; it is useful to have as you repair your credit report. This type of request ensures credit reporting companies adhere with the law while conducting an investigation. Since most of the investigations are actually automated, a request for a Method of Verification alerts the companies to the fact that they're dealing with a savvy consumer.

Unfortunately, credit bureaus don't often follow the law entirely when it comes to obtaining verifiable information. They often don't adhere to the FCRA law. Fortunately, you are able to force their hand into doing so. In this way, you can remove negative, unverifiable information permanently from your credit report.

Using this method to repair your credit report is not just saying that the negative items aren't yours or that they're inaccurate. It claims that the credit bureaus don't comply with the law and therefore must delete any unverifiable items. If this isn't done, then you, the consumer, can file an official complaint with the Federal Trade Commission.

Financial advisors often have situations where they try to remove judgments for their clients. They can write more than 1 or 2 dispute letters. If they write that they are taking things further up the line to the Federal Trade Commission, then the disputes are usually handled quicker and easier. This means – DO NOT GIVE UP. Credit bureaus must delete items that can't be verified satisfactorily.

This verification method request should be done after a dispute letter has been sent and you have received either a "Verified: or a "New Information Below" reply from a credit bureau.

Never utilize an electronic dispute on a credit bureau website on the Internet.

If you do so you will have relinquished a lot of necessary and very important rights. One of the conditions on their website you will be agreeing to is that any disputed item which comes back as "verified" will mean you cannot re-dispute it ever again and you lose the right to do so.

Another thing you'll need is your certified letter including the delivery confirmation should you decide to file an official complaint using the Fair Trade Commission. In most cases, credit bureaus would rather remove all the items mentioned in your letter instead of wasting time and effort dealing with the Fair Trade Commission.

CHAPTER 7: STEPS YOU CAN TAKE TO ENSURE ALL NEGATIVE ITEMS ARE REMOVED

Stick to the following steps:

Step No. 1: Dispute Letter Format

You will write a letter of dispute then send it out to every bureau (Addresses were provided above in the previous chapter).

You must send one of these letters to every one of the major credit bureaus – TransUnion, Experian and Equifax. You don't want to go to the trouble of having an item deleted in one of the bureaus and later have it come up on another one.

DON'T USE INTERNET TEMPLATES FOR YOUR LETTER.

You must know that credit bureaus scan your letters using a computer program. If a type of Internet template is used (and they usually are), the bureau is able to stop an investigation even before it arrives at its destination. Then you'll receive a letter of denial with some frivolous reason.

It's better for you to hand write the dispute in black or blue pen, or alter the sample below a little and use your own words.

SAMPLE DISPUTE LETTER:

Name and Address
City, & State, Zip
Date of Birth & Social Security Number
[Credit Bureau Name here]
Address of credit bureau
City, State, Zip Code
Date
RE: The inaccurate information appearing on my credit report. Social Security No. _____

I am writing to dispute the listed accounts below:
1. Chase, Account #4545454
2. First National bank, Charge off account #4545454

I am requesting a deletion of this information from my credit file due to inaccuracies regarding this information. I formally request this information be deleted from my credit report file.
 I am also requesting that a description of procedures used to determine accuracy and completeness of all information is provided to me within 15 days of your completing your reinvestigation. As per federal law, you now have 30 days to conclude your re-investigation.

Thanking you kindly for your assistance with this matter.

Yours Sincerely,
(Signature)
Your Name

The average time is around 30 days to get a response but sometimes it can be as early as 20 days or as late as 40 days. The credit bureau might respond with a "Deleted" letter and this would be the best-case scenario.

If one of the Bureaus has deleted the items but the others have not, then write only a Step 2 letter to bureaus, which sent you an explanation or a verified letter. Don't write back to the bureau about the deleted items

The one thing you don't want to do is have an investigation reopened. The only time you will need to write back is if a credit bureau has had some of the accounts deleted but others not. Then write about Step 2 only and write about any undeleted items.

There was an individual who had 18 negative items on his report. One of the bureaus sent him 13 "deleted," 2 items "verified." The bureau neglected one of the items altogether.

He had to send a round 2 Method of Verification letter, which only tackled the 2 verified items, as well as the neglected one. There was no need to mention the rest of them that were deleted, as they had been dealt with satisfactorily.

Step 2: Verification Letter Format and Sample

Name
Address
City/State/Zip Code
Date
RE: Request to provide Method of Verification

Dear Sir/Madam

On [Write Original Dispute Date] I had requested an investigation believing the item isn't being legally reported. On [Write Date of Response] I received a letter from you stating that the investigation had been concluded and was complete. I ask that you please answer these questions:
Which certified documents did you review in order to conduct your investigation?
I ask that you please provide complete copies of all information which was transmitted to the data furnisher as part of the investigation, as is required by the Fair Credit Reporting Act.
Please detail: Who you spoke with - What was the date - How long the conversation was - What was the person's position - What number you called - The name of your employee who spoke to the creditor - What your employee's position is that spoke to the creditor.
The inaccurate reporting from you has caused me both emotional and financial distress.

Please reply to the questions above within 15 days, or delete these items.

Yours Sincerely,
Name
Date of Birth
Social Security Number and Address

Step3: Example Letter of complaint with the Fair Trade Commission

If you send the second letter and still don't get a satisfactory response, send another letter, a third one. This will be your letter of intent to complain to the Fair Trade Commission if the particular issue isn't resolved.

Name and Address
Credit Bureau Department and Credit Bureau Address
Date
RE: Follow-up Dispute Letter of (write date of the original validation request letter)

NOTICE OF INTENT TO FILE A COMPLAINT
Dear Sir/Madam

This is a formal letter advising you of my intention to file an official complaint with the Fair Trade Commission because of your disregard for the law.

You have claimed to have verified the specific items that I requested. I therefore legally requested that you send me a clear description of all the procedures you utilized to verify this information.

As shown by the attached copy of the letter and mailing receipt [Insert Date on Receipt], you accepted and received my request letter by registered mail dated [Insert Date of Your Letter]. You have not responded to this request and have thus not performed your duty according to the law, which requires you to respond within 15 days. You have not responded and it has now been more than 30 days. Any failure to comply with federal regulations by credit reporting agencies will be investigated by the Federal Trade Commission (see 15 USC 41, et seq.). Be advised that I am keeping careful records of all communication with you regarding this matter in order to then file an official complaint through the Fair Trade Commission, if I do not hear from you within 20 days.

The information below is mistakenly contained on my personal credit report.

[List all the company name(s) and also account number(s) here]

You have stated that you have verified this erroneous information, however, you do not tell me exactly HOW you verified these accounts. Please remove this incomplete or inaccurate information from my file immediately or I will be filing a formal complaint through the Fair Trade Commission. As mentioned above, I am documenting all these events carefully and this includes your lack of response, which is REQUIRED according to federal law.

Yours Sincerely,
Name
Social Security Number

It would be very unusual if you have to go any further than that. Just letting them know about your intention to file an official complaint through the Fair Trade Commission should work. In the rare case that it doesn't work, you can always file a complaint at the FTC and allow an investigation to begin.

Remember to have patience. It will all be worth it when you see credit card offers arrive in the mail with a zero percent interest rate, along with offers from car dealers and others. At that point it will become clear that your credit has been fixed, you are categorized as being a low risk customer, and you have become credit worthy.

Sometimes, it might be worth writing to the credit bureaus a second time instead of going with the method of verification letter. You could advise them in a clear manner that all information by the Fair Credit Reporting Act has to be completely accurate 100% and at this point it still is not. The bureaus must respond in a period of 30 days. They receive around 10,000 letters per day and of course, cannot respond to every one of them. Therefore, they delete items.

In some cases, attorneys will send letters of dispute several times and wait from 3 to 7 days between sending each one. This can work too, but method of verification letters are better in most cases.

CHAPTER 8: HOW TO HANDLE COLLECTION AGENCIES

Many people often think that if they make even a smaller payment to creditors that are harassing them, they will stay off their back. Harassment will occur when collection agencies or creditors realize the statute of limitations in your particular state is approaching and are eager to get any amount of money from you. This way they can keep your debt "alive" so to speak. Be aware that every state has different periods, which apply to the statute of limitations.

What this means is that if you've got credit card debt, for example, and your particular state has a three-year statute of limitations, if the three-year mark is approaching and you pay only fifty cents to a creditor then you begin a new three-year statute of limitations. If you do this then creditors can continue to sue you for three more years. However, if you haven't paid the creditors anything during the three years and then the creditor decides to sue you, it could be thrown out of court if you prove the statute of limitations has passed.

Another option would be to send a letter (a certified one) to the lawyer who is suing you and ask him/her to stop the suit immediately as the statute of limitations has passed in your particular state.

You could also request proof of debt validation from the particular collection agency as another way of stopping the agency from harassing you. They will have to provide that within 30 days according to the law.

CHAPTER 9: ANOTHER METHOD OF LEGALLY REMOVING NEGATIVE ITEMS

Debt Validation Letter
You can challenge the legitimacy of a debt collection agency claims you owe through the Federal Debt Collection Practices Act. People do not request proof of debt validation from collection agencies even though the agencies don't often keep written copies of debt contracts. What usually happens is that the agencies buy debts for just a few pennies or a dollar.

So, if you're being sued or harassed by a collection agency, write a letter to them requesting debt validation proof. The lawsuits and/or phone calls will likely cease. This doesn't mean, however, that you don't owe money anymore but that you have some breathing space until the information you requested is given to you.

If you are sent a computerized printout, don't accept it. The only thing that is acceptable is your written contract which contains your signature, amount, date and all other detailed information. Without this, a creditor cannot take you to court and sue you, nor can they contact you again unless they provide a written contract with the abovementioned information on it.

Below is a sample letter to a collection agency. Ensure the agency verifies that this debt is yours and you owe it. Make sure you keep another copy of the letter on file for yourself. Send your letter by registered mail and also make sure you get a receipt of delivery.

Step 1: Sample Letter to a Collection Agency

Date
From: Your Name
Address
City, State Zip Code
To: Collection Agency Name
Agency Address
City, State Zip

Regarding: Account # 1111-1111-1111-1111

Dear Sir/Madam

I am writing to respond to your letter dated ---- . Please be advised that I am not refusing to pay, however, this is a notice in accordance with the Fair Debt Collection Practices Act, 15 USC 1692g Sec. 809 (b). I am disputing your claim and request validation.

Please be advised, I am not asking for a 'verification' request or proof of my mailing address. It is a VALIDATION request following the abovementioned Title and the abovementioned Section. I ask that you provide clear evidence showing I am legally obliged to pay you.

I ask that you provide:

1. What the money you state I owe you is for;
2. An explanation and clear display of how exactly you calculated the amount you claim I owe you;
3. Provide copies of papers that are clear in showing I agreed to pay that which you claim I owe;
4. Identify the original creditor;
5. Provide verification or copies of any judgments if applicable;
6. Provide proof that the Statute of Limitations hasn't elapsed on this particular account;
7. Provide proof that you are licensed and can collect in my particular state;
8. Provide your license number and proof that you are a Registered Agent.

If your office has reported any inaccurate information to any one of the 3 main Credit Bureaus (TransUnion Equifax, or Experian), said action may be considered fraud under State and Federal Laws. If negative marks by your own company or a company you represent, are found on my credit reports, I will bring legal action against you for:

Defamation of Character

Violation of the Fair Debt Collection Practices Act and Violation of the Fair Credit Reporting Act

If you provide the documentation requested, I require 30 days at least to investigate the information provided. During this time any collection activity has to cease and desist.

In addition, if any type of action is taken that could be deemed detrimental to any one of my credit reports during this validation period, I will be getting legal advice from my counsel. This would include any information that goes to credit reporting repositories that may be invalidated, inaccurate or verifying a particular account as accurate when there is no proof provided that it actually is.

If your office does not respond to this request for validation within 30 days from the date of your receipt, you must remove and delete all references to this account completely from my credit file. You must also send a copy of this deletion request to me.

I am also requesting within this letter that your offices make no contact with me by telephone either at my workplace or my home. If your office attempts any communication by phone with me, including but not limited to correspondence sent to any third parties or computer created calls, it will be deemed harassment and I will be forced to file suit. All communications with me from this point on MUST be in writing and sent to the address appearing in this letter.

This is a bid to correct your records and any information that is obtained will be utilized for that specific purpose.

Yours Sincerely
Signature
 Your Name

Step 2:

After you have requested a debt validation letter from the particular collection agency but haven't received one, you will write another letter to the specific collection agency and request an item be removed from your credit report, because they are violating the Fair Debt Collection Practices Act, section 809 (b).

Step 3:

(Do this step only if a collection agency does not remove the item in question.)
If a collection agency doesn't reply to the request you sent to remove an item, do the following:

- Contact the particular credit bureau
- Write a letter to this credit bureau and request they remove the particular item from your credit report, and include a copy of the original letter that you sent to that creditor asking for the removal of the item as no proof of validation was given.

It is preferable to work with the particular credit bureau directly, instead of dealing with creditors or collection agencies. It generally works best. Keep on being persistent as the credit bureaus must then permanently erase the negative items. You may need to write another letter, however, it is usually the case that after receiving an FTC letter of complaint and warning, they will have the items deleted.

Do not forget that credit bureaus receive around 10,000 letters each day and that they are profit-making organizations. They like to be cost effective and as fast as possible. This is why complaints are sent abroad to countries with cheaper labor. That's also why they use e-Oscar, their electronic system.

Credit bureaus who realize they've got a savvy consumer to deal with would rather erase an item instead of risk having to deal with a complaint and going through to the Fair Trade Commission.

Considering credit bureaus don't follow the rules of the FCRA and often don't provide legitimate and solid proof to consumers in the majority of cases, you should be able to have all negative items deleted from your credit report in a legal and permanent manner. Another thing you can do is actually sue them considering they are violating the FDCPA for $1000.

CHAPTER 10: WHAT MISTAKES YOU SHOULD AVOID WHEN FIXING YOUR CREDIT

1. Don't give additional information or details to credit bureaus regarding a negative item. As an example – don't write that a collection agency shows $1300, but that you only owe only $300. Credit bureaus may change a sum, however the particular item will remain. Remember that bureaus must have totally accurate information. An item showing $1300 and not $300 is obviously inaccurate therefore you only need to write, "this particular item is inaccurate."

2. Make sure all mail is certified; with the delivery return receipts for all correspondence you have had with any credit bureau. If you ever file a lawsuit or claim, you should have a paper trail showing proof that you did indeed send a claim.

3. Keep copies of correspondence between you and the bureau.

4. Never use electronic dispute requests on the websites of credit bureaus. If you do this you are essentially giving up all your rights because you agree to their terms and therefore surrender your rights. When items are verified or denied you cannot re-dispute them ever again. Credit bureaus don't need to respond in writing to you. Case closed. Perhaps it may seem more comfortable however, it is indeed very costly. Use old-fashioned ways of correspondence - letters.

5. Don't close the credit cards you do not need. Your individual debt ratio is likely to rise, possibly resulting in your actual credit score being reduced. Keep all your accounts open and use them for only very small amounts each month. Pay for the accounts fully when a statement is sent to you.

6. Pay credit cards fully each month if you can. This shows you are actually a lower risk type consumer who can manage finances.

7. Ask credit card companies to extend the credit limit line for you. If a credit company needs to do a credit check - skip it as this could affect your FICO score.

8. Don't use templates from the Internet for your disputes. If you do, they could be denied and classed as trivial by credit bureaus before even reaching their destination. It's best to use a reliable sample but changing the wording. You could also use the samples provided here but make sure to change the wording to ensure it's accurate with your situation.

9. Ensure you check your individual credit once each year at least. Remember, this is free. This way you can ensure you know exactly what's on your credit report. It could be that you discover some new items in time and fix them.

10. Make sure you re-establish your credit. People often fail to do this. If a company refuses you a credit card, you can find a bank or credit company that

allows you to put money into an account, then extend a line of credit for the same amount. Ask the bank or credit company to report this to all credit bureaus. This way you'll show a revolving and open borrowing capacity.

Please remember: Don't give up quickly! Keep trying. Sometimes all that is needed is one more letter. The average is one or two letters (particularly if you mention complaining to the Fair Trade Commission or going to a lawyer) and sometimes three letters.

THANKS FOR READING

We really hope you enjoyed this book. If you found this material helpful feel free to share it with friends. You can also help others find it by leaving a review where you purchased the book. Your feedback will help us continue to write books you love.

The Smart Reads library is growing by the day! Make sure and check out the other wonderful books in our catalog. We would love to hear which books are your favorite.

Visit:
www.smartreads.co/freebooks
to receive Smart Reads books for FREE

Check us out on Instagram:
www.instagram.com/smart_readers
@smart_readers

Don't forget your 2 FREE audiobooks.
Use this link www.audibletrial.com/Travis to claim your 2 FREE Books.

SMART READS ORIGINS

Smart Reads was born out of the desire to find the best information fast without having to wade through the sheer volume of fluff available online. Smart Reads combs through massive amounts of knowledge compiles the best into quick to read books on a variety of subjects.

We consider ourselves Smart Readers, not dummies. We know reading is smart. We're self taught. We like to learn a TON about a WIDE variety of topics. We have developed a love for books and we find intelligence attractive.

We found that each new topic we tried to learn about started with the challenge of finding the pieces of the puzzle that mattered most. It becomes a treasure hunt rather than an education.

Smart Reads wants to find the best of the best information for you. To condense it into a package that you can consume in an hour or less. So you can read more books about more topics in less time.

OUR MISSION

Smart Reads aims to accelerate the availability of useful information and will publish a high quality book on every major topic on amazon.

Smart Reads hopes to remove barriers to sharing by taking the copyright off everything we publish and donating it to the public domain. We hope other publishers and authors will follow our example.

Our goal is to donate $1,000,000 or more by 2020 to build over 2,000 schools by giving 5% of our net profit to Pencils of Promise.

We want to restore forests around the globe by planting a tree for every 10 physical books we sell and hope to plant over 100,000 trees by 2020.

Doesn't it feel good knowing that by educating yourself you are helping the world be a better place? We think so too…

Thanks for helping us help the world. You Smart Reader you…

Travis and the Smart Reads Team

WHY I STARTED SMART READS

Every time I wanted to learn about something new I'd have to buy 20 books on the topic and spend way too long sorting through them and reading them all until I arrived at the big picture. Until I had enough perspectives to know who was just guessing, who was uninformed and who had stumbled upon something remarkable.

I wished someone else could just go in and figure that out for me and tell me what matters. That's how smart reads was born. I want smart reads to be a company that does all that research up front. Sorts through all the content that is available on each topic and pulls out the most up to date complete understanding, then have people smarter than me package the best wisdom in an easy to understand way in the least amount of words possible.

For example, I got a new puppy so I wanted to learn about dog training. I bought 14 different books about dog training and by the time I got through the first 5 and finally started getting the big picture on the best way to train my puppy she had grown up into a dog.

Yeah she's well behaved. She doesn't poop in the house. I can get her to sit and come when I call. But what if someone else went in and read all those books for me, found the underlying themes and picked out the best information that would give me the big picture and get me right to the point. And I'd only have to read one book instead of 15.

That would be amazing. I would save time. And maybe my dog would be rolling over, cleaning up after my kids and doing the dishes by now. That my friend, is the reason I started smart reads. Because I wanted a company I can trust to deliver me the best information in an easy to understand way that I can digest in under an hour. Because dog training is one of many subjects I want to master.

The quicker I can learn a wide variety of topics the sooner that information can begin playing a role in shaping my future. And none of us knows how long that future will be. So why not do everything we can to make the best of it and consume a ton of knowledge. And I figured all the better if I can also make a positive difference in the world.

That's why we're also building schools, planting trees and challenging ideas about copyright's place in today's world. Because as a company we have to be doing everything we can to support the ecosystem that gives us all these beautiful places to read our books. Thanks for reading.

Travis

Customers Who Bought This Customers Who Bought This Book Also Bought

Passive Income: Do What You Want When You Want and Make Money While You Sleep

Develop Self-Discipline: Daily Habit to Make Self Confidence and Will Power Automatic

Blockchain Revolution: Understanding the Internet of Money

The Everything Store Sales Guide: How to Make Money with Amazon FBA

Success Principles: Techniques for Positive Thinking, Self Love and Developing a Powerful

Understanding Affiliate Marketing: An Internet Marketing Guide for How To Make Money Online Using Products, Websites and Services

Mastering Your Time: Learn How Successful People Enhance Productivity, Beat Procrastination and Do More in Less Time

A Detailed Guide in Building A Successful Photography Business Online: Learn How to Market, Sell, Promote and Make Money as a Photographer

www.ingramcontent.com/pod-product-compliance
Lightning Source LLC
Chambersburg PA
CBHW061447180526
45170CB00004B/1594